Prayer Book
for the Year of Consecrated Life

by Donal Anthony Foley

*All booklets are published thanks to the
generous support of the members of the
Catholic Truth Society*

CATHOLIC TRUTH SOCIETY

PUBLISHERS TO THE HOLY SEE

Contents

ISBN 978 1 78469 024 3

PART ONE

~ HISTORY AND DEVELOPMENT ~
OF CONSECRATED LIFE

~ Introduction ~

On 29th November 2013, during the 82nd General Assembly of the Union of Superior Generals of religious orders, Pope Francis announced that the year 2015 would be dedicated to consecrated life, and specifically its mission and identity. He said that, "A radical approach is required of all Christians, but religious persons are called upon to follow the Lord in a special way: they are men and women who can awaken the world."

On 31st January 2014, Cardinal João Braz De Aviz, the Prefect of the Congregation for Institutes of Consecrated Life and Societies of Apostolic Life, said that the Year will take place in the context of the 50th anniversary of the Second Vatican Council: "We believe that the Council has been a breath of the Spirit not only for the whole Church but, perhaps especially, for the consecrated life."

He went on to say that the first objective of this Year would be to "make a grateful remembrance of the recent past," while its second objective will be to "embrace the future with hope." He emphasised the third objective, that of "living the present with passion": a passion which requires love, true friendship and profound communion. In addition, he said that the Year of

Consecrated Life will focus on "the beauty of following Christ," in an evangelical sense, in the various types of religious vocations. The Year is expected to begin in late 2014, and close in November 2015.

Consecrated Life in the Church today

We can ask if the consecrated life is still relevant for the Church, especially when we hear so much nowadays about the new lay movements and communities. It might be argued that these can take the place of religious orders and congregations, and that specific vows of poverty, chastity and obedience are no longer necessary.

It is certainly true that lay movements and communities have come to the fore in recent years, as part of the New Evangelisation promoted in particular by Pope St John Paul II. But that doesn't mean that the religious orders and congregations have become irrelevant. Rather we can see here the action of the Holy Spirit who has raised up these new movements to enable the Church to evangelise more effectively under the particular circumstances of modern life.

But there will always be a need for religious orders and congregations to give witness to the importance of the evangelical counsels for the Church, that is the ideals of poverty, chastity and obedience, in line with two thousand years of Catholic tradition.

It is also important that they give witness to the whole Church - a Church in which every Christian is called to be perfect as the heavenly Father is perfect - that such an ideal of perfection is possible and attainable in the modern world. Although ordinary Catholics are not specifically called to live these counsels in the fullest sense, nevertheless they are meant to live their spirit insofar as this is compatible with their state of life.

It is also worth noting that many of the best known individuals over the last century or so that the Church has declared to be saints - that is those who we should particularly be emulating - have been religious. These include figures such as St Thérèse of Lisieux, the Carmelite nun who was canonised in 1925, or St Maximilian Kolbe, the Franciscan martyr of Auschwitz who died in 1941 and St Padre Pio, also a Franciscan, who was canonised in 2002.

More recently still, we have the example of Blessed Mother Teresa of Calcutta, who died in 1997, and whose Missionaries of Charity Order has thousands of members who are active in many countries, and who have given a wonderful Christian witness both to Catholics and the world generally.

For all these reasons, we can say that consecrated life is still very relevant for the Church today.

What is Consecrated Life?

There are some foreshadowings of the way the consecrated life would develop in the Church in the Bible. In St Matthew's Gospel, towards the end of Jesus's earthly ministry, he warned his disciples about the danger of riches. This was after he had spoken to the rich young man who kept the commandments but was unwilling to give up his wealth and follow Jesus unreservedly.

This prompted St Peter to ask what the reward would be for those disciples who *had* left everything and followed him. In reply, Jesus promised them thrones in his heavenly kingdom, before saying: "And every one who has left houses or brothers or sisters or father or mother or children or lands, for my name's sake, will receive a hundredfold, and inherit eternal life." (*Mt* 19:29)

So here we have a sense that in Christ's future community, the Church, some of his disciples would give up everything to follow him, and thus be richly rewarded. This is what the consecrated life is essentially about - a special following of Christ, a special dedication or consecration to him, above and beyond that required of ordinary Christians.

We can see an outline of what became the evangelical counsels, that is poverty, chastity and obedience, in this quote from the *Catechism*: "In the three synoptic Gospels, Jesus's call to the rich young man to follow him, in the obedience of a disciple and in the observance of the Commandments, is joined to a call to poverty and chastity" (*CCC* 1973, 1974, 2053). The evangelical counsels are thus a call to perfection, to go beyond the basic precepts or teaching of Jesus.

According to the *Catechism*, the consecrated life undeniably belongs to the life and holiness of the Church (914), and while all are called to perfection, those who are specially vowed to God, in the practise of poverty, chastity and obedience, and solemnly profess these evangelical counsels in a permanent state of life recognised by the Church, are living a life characteristic of consecration to God (915).

The Beginnings of Consecrated Life

However, consecrated life as we know it was difficult to live during the first three centuries of the Church's life, due to the severe outbreaks of persecution it had to endure as the Roman Empire sought to destroy Christianity. It was only from the time of the Emperor Constantine onwards that the Church was able to live more freely, thus allowing early forms of consecrated life for individuals and religious communities to develop.

Initially, the impetus for this was a desire to emulate the martyrs, and this led some of the early Christians to move to desert areas, particularly in Egypt and parts of Syria, so as to live a more penitential and thus perfect life. They were the first hermits, those living the *eremitical* or solitary life, which comes from the Greek word for desert, *eremos*.

St Antony (c. 251-356) was the first great leader of this movement, and it is worth noting that when he embarked on his desert vocation he entrusted his sister to the care of a group of Christian virgins living a primitive form of religious life. Indeed, over time, it was recognised that living in community was better for most people than being on their own. Gradually Christian monastic-style communities developed in Egypt, under St Pachomius (c. 292-348).

St Gregory of Nyssa (c. 335-c. 395), wrote a life of his sister, St Macrina (c. 330-379), detailing how she had founded a convent and monastery on the family estates in what is now Turkey, with the help of her younger brother. Indeed we could say that consecrated life developed out of lay people deciding to live a more dedicated form of life in their own homes.

It may well be that some of the new lay movements in the modern Church will develop into consecrated forms of life over time, and then it would be a case of history repeating itself.

Be that as it may, St Basil the Great, (c. 330-379), formulated a monastic rule in the fourth century for the Eastern Church, and he was followed in the West by St Benedict (c. 480-543), whose rule had an immense influence from the sixth century onwards. The Benedictine rule has a focus on *obedience*, and this was important at a time when society was in a state of upheaval following the collapse of the Roman Empire.

The Growth of Consecrated Life

But by the thirteenth century, as society became more urban, the monasteries had become remote from the people. Thus developed the mendicant orders, such as the Franciscans and Dominicans: they lived a different form of consecrated life in their friaries, one closer to the ordinary people, and more suited to life in the growing towns. St Francis of Assisi's focus on *poverty* was also a counterbalance to the growing wealth of the Church and society at this time.

In the sixteenth century, in the wake of the Reformation, a new type of religious life, as exemplified by the Jesuits, was needed, with less emphasis on the common life as usually found in monastic houses or friaries, and more of a focus on the work of evangelisation, education and charitable activities generally. As in the case of the situation in St Benedict's time, the post-Reformation period was a time of upheaval, and so St Ignatius of Loyola, the founder of the Jesuits, also placed much emphasis on the idea of *obedience*, even formulating a fourth vow of special obedience to the Pope.

These types of apostolic institutes experienced great growth in the nineteenth century, with some congregations focusing on charitable work, and others on evangelisation. The Salesian Religious Institute, founded by St John Bosco, and dedicated to the education of the young, is one such example of a nineteenth century foundation. Other forms of consecrated life are also possible, for example for modern hermits or consecrated widows.

Consecrated Life today

Although numerous lay communities and societies have grown up in the Church, particularly since the Second Vatican Council, consecrated life, as found in the various orders and religious institutes, is still of great importance for the Church in carrying the Gospel to the world and in bearing witness to Christ.

Those living the consecrated life, also provide an example to the laity of the importance of living the Christian life generously. And even if most lay people cannot follow them literally in the practises of poverty, chastity and obedience, they can live the evangelical counsels in spirit, in terms of a more frugal life, with a focus on helping the poor; in living chastely in either the married or single life; and in obediently following the teachings of the Church.

And we should realise that according to St Thomas Aquinas the perfection of the Church on earth requires the three states of the laity, the ordained priesthood, and the consecrated life. So in that sense the consecrated life is essential for the Church, and that is why it has always been so highly prized.

Recent Church and Papal teaching on the Consecrated Life

In recent times, important documents relating to the consecrated life have come out of the Second Vatican Council and papal teaching, as in the case of the Vatican II document, *Perfectae Caritatis* which was issued as a decree for the adaptation and renewal of religious life by Pope Paul VI in October 1965.

Nearly twenty years later, in March 1984, Pope St John Paul II issued his Apostolic Exhortation, *Redemptionis Donum*, which was addressed to men and women religious, and concerned with their consecration in the light of the mystery of the redemption.

Following this, in March 1996, he issued *Vita Consecrata*, his post-synodal Apostolic Exhortation on the consecrated life and its mission in the Church and the world. In this he emphasised the importance of this way of life for the Church, saying:

> *The Consecrated Life, deeply rooted in the example and teaching of Christ the Lord, is a gift of God the Father to his Church through the Holy Spirit. By the profession of the evangelical counsels the characteristic features of Jesus - the chaste, poor and obedient one - are made constantly 'visible' in the midst of the world and the eyes of the faithful are directed towards the mystery of the Kingdom of God already at work in history, even as it awaits its full realisation in heaven.*

The following year, on the Feast of the Presentation of the Lord, 2nd February 1997, Pope St John Paul II instituted a "World Day of Prayer for Consecrated Life", which has been celebrated annually ever since, in thanksgiving to God for the gift to the Church of the consecrated life in its different forms.

Pope Benedict XVI also strongly supported the consecrated life, and preached homilies for the annual World Day of Prayer, while Pope Francis has continued this tradition, and has now dedicated 2015 as the Year of Consecrated Life.

PART TWO

~ PRAYERS, REFLECTIONS ~
AND SCRIPTURAL
READINGS RELATED
TO CONSECRATED LIFE

~ Prayers for Vocations ~
to the Consecrated Life
and Priesthood

Since Christ himself said, with reference to the need to pray for vocations, "The harvest is rich but the labourers are few, so ask the Lord of the harvest to send labourers to his harvest," we can be sure that God values such prayers very highly.

L oving God, you call all who believe in you
to grow perfect in love by following in the footsteps
of Christ your Son.
Call from among us more men and women
who will serve you as religious.
By their way of life, may they provide a convincing sign
of your Kingdom for the Church and the whole world.
We ask this in Jesus's name.
Amen.

O Father, you desire all of us to be happy.
Stir up the grace of a religious vocation in the hearts
of many men and women.
Grant to them the willingness and generosity

to give of themselves, their lives, their time and their
talents to the service of Jesus Christ,
Your Son, Our Lord and Saviour,
and to His Holy Church.

L ord Jesus Christ, Saviour of the world, show forth,
we beseech Thee, in Thy Church the Holy Spirit with
whose power the apostles were so abundantly filled. We
thank Thee for the blessings bestowed upon the work of
priests and religious; and we pray that Thou wilt add to
the number of those who now pray, labour and sacrifice
themselves for Thy glory and the salvation of souls. Give
them unselfish zeal for Thy glory. O good Jesus, give
us more priests and religious after Thine own Heart!
Amen.

Prayer for Chastity

O my God, teach me to love others with the purity of
your holy Mother. Give me the grace to resist firmly
every temptation to impure thoughts, words or actions.
Teach me always to love with generosity and goodness,
to respect myself and others in the way I act and to
reverence the way you have given us for the creation of
new life.

～ Prayers of the Saints ～
Concerning Consecrated Life

After we have prayed to the Lord of the Harvest for vocations to the consecrated life, we should also pray to the Saints, many of whom have been religious, with this important intention in mind.

Prayers of St Benedict of Nursia, founder of the Benedictine Order

O gracious and holy One,
give us the wisdom to perceive you,
intelligence to understand you,
diligence to seek you,
patience to wait for you,
eyes to behold you,
a heart to meditate on you,
and a life to proclaim you.

O Lord, I place myself in your hands and dedicate myself to you. I pledge myself to do your will in all things: To love the Lord God with all my heart, all my soul, all my strength. Not to kill. Not to steal. Not to covet. Not to bear false witness. To honour all persons. Not to do to another what I would not wish done to myself. To chastise the body. Not to seek after pleasures. To love fasting. To relieve the poor. To clothe the naked. To visit the sick. To bury the dead. To help in trouble. To console the sorrowing. To hold myself aloof from worldly ways. To prefer nothing to the love of Christ. Not to give way to anger. Not to foster a desire for revenge. Not to entertain deceit in the heart. Not to make a false peace. Not to forsake charity. Not to swear, lest I swear falsely. To speak the truth with heart and tongue. Not to return evil for evil. To do no injury: yea, even to bear patiently any injury done to me. To love my enemies. Not to curse those who curse me, but rather to bless them. To bear persecution for justice's sake. Not to be proud. Not to be given to intoxicating drink. Not to be an over-eater. Not to be lazy. Not to be slothful. Not to be a murmurer. Not to be a detractor. To put my trust in God. To refer the good I see in myself to God. To refer any evil in myself to myself. To fear the Day of Judgement. To be in dread of hell. To desire eternal life with spiritual longing. To keep death before my eyes daily. To keep constant watch over my actions. To remember that God sees me everywhere. To call upon Christ for defence against evil thoughts that arise in my heart. To guard my tongue against wicked speech. To avoid much speaking. To avoid idle talk. To read only what is good to read. To look at only what is good to see. To pray often. To ask forgiveness daily for my sins, and to seek ways to amend my life. To obey my superiors in all things rightful. Not to desire to be thought holy, but to seek holiness. To fulfil the commandments of God by good works. To love chastity. To hate no one. Not to be jealous or envious of anyone. Not to love strife. Not to love pride. To honour the aged. To pray for my enemies. To make peace after a quarrel, before the setting of the sun. Never to despair of your mercy, O God of Mercy. Amen.

Prayer to St Francis of Assisi, the founder of the Franciscan Order

O God, who, through the merits of blessed Francis, didst give increase to Thy Church,
by enriching her with new offspring:
grant us, that following his example
we may despise earthly goods
and ever rejoice in partaking of Thy heavenly gifts.
Through our Lord Jesus Christ, Thy Son,
Who lives and reigns with You and Holy Spirit,
one God, for ever and ever.
Amen.

Prayer to St Clare of Assisi

God of mercy, You inspired St Clare with the love of poverty. By the help of her prayers may we follow Christ in poverty of spirit and come to the joyful vision of Your glory in the Kingdom of heaven. We ask this through Our Lord Jesus Christ, Your Son, Who lives and reigns with you and the Holy Spirit, one God, forever and ever. Amen.

Prayer of St Teresa of Avila

Let nothing disturb you,
Let nothing frighten you,
All things are passing away:
God never changes.
Patience obtains all things
Whoever has God lacks nothing;
God alone suffices.

Prayers of St Ignatius of Loyola, the founder of the Jesuits

Teach us, good Lord, to serve you as you deserve; to give and not to count the cost; to fight and not to heed the wounds; to toil and not to seek for rest; to labour and not to ask for any reward, save that of knowing that we do your will.

Take, O Lord, my entire liberty,
   Accept my memory,
   my understanding and my whole will.
Whatsoever I have or possess comes from your bounty.
I render it all back to you, and submit it to the
   governance of your will.
Grant me but your love and your grace,
   and I am rich indeed,
nor do I ask for ought besides.

O Christ Jesus
   When all is darkness
And we feel our weakness and helplessness,
Give us the sense of Your Presence,
Your Love and Your Strength.
Help us to have perfect trust
In Your protecting love
And strengthening power,
So that nothing may frighten or worry us,
For, living close to You,
We shall see Your Hand,
Your Purpose, Your Will through all things.

St Thérèse of Lisieux

O my God! I offer Thee all my actions of this day for the intentions and for the glory of the Sacred Heart of Jesus. I desire to sanctify every beat of my heart, my every thought, my simplest works, by uniting them to its infinite merits; and I wish to make reparation for my sins by casting them into the furnace of its merciful love. O my God! I ask of Thee for myself and for those whom I hold dear, the grace to fulfil perfectly Thy holy will, to accept for love of Thee the joys and sorrows of this passing life, so that we may one day be united together in heaven for all eternity. Amen.

~ Papal Prayers for Religious ~

The Popes, as leaders of the Catholic Church on earth, have been very conscious of the need to pray for vocations to the religious life, knowing that such vocations are very precious for the Church.

Pope Paul VI

Father, every good intention has its origin and fulfilment in you. Guide your people along the path of salvation and look kindly on those who have left all things to follow Christ in chastity, poverty and obedience and to consecrate themselves to you. In their service to you, Father, and to all their brothers and sisters, may they give faithful witness to Christ. Through the same Christ our Lord. Amen.

(From *Pope's Family Prayer Book*,
Libreria Editrice Vaticana, 1975)

Pope St John Paul II

Lord, Jesus Christ, Good Shepherd of our souls, You who know Your sheep and know how to reach the human heart...Stir the hearts of those young people who would follow You but who cannot overcome doubts and fears, and who in the end follow other voices and other paths which lead nowhere. You who are the Word of the Father, the Word which creates and saves, the Word which enlightens and sustains hearts - conquer with Your Spirit the resistance and delays of indecisive hearts. Arouse in those whom You call the courage of love's answer: "Here I am, send me."

Lord Jesus, as you once called the first disciples, let your sweet invitation continue to resound: Come follow me! Give young men and women the grace of responding quickly to your voice.

Awaken in our community a missionary eagerness. Lord, send workers to your harvest and do not allow humanity to be lost for the lack of pastors, missionaries, and people dedicated to the cause of the Gospel. Mary, Mother of the Church, the model of every vocation, help us to say "yes" to the Lord who calls us to co-operate in the divine plan of salvation. Amen.

Novenas for
~ Consecrated Life ~

Novenas, that is prayers usually prayed over a period of nine days for a particular intention, have been popular in the Church for centuries. The following novenas are directed to the Holy Spirit, and can be prayed with intentions focusing on vocation and consecration.

Novena to the Holy Spirit for the Seven Gifts

Act of Consecration to the Holy Spirit

On my knees before the great multitude of heavenly witnesses, I offer myself, soul and body to You, Eternal Spirit of God. I adore the brightness of Your purity, the unerring keenness of Your justice and the might of Your love. You are the Strength and Light of my soul. In You I live and move and am. I desire never to grieve You by unfaithfulness to grace and I pray with all my heart to be kept from the smallest sin against You. Mercifully guard my every thought and grant that I may always watch for Your light, and listen to Your voice, and follow Your gracious inspirations. I cling to You and give myself to You and ask You, by Your compassion to watch over me in my weakness. Holding the pierced Feet of

Jesus and looking at His Five Wounds, and trusting in His Precious Blood and adoring His opened Side and stricken Heart, I implore You, Adorable Spirit, Helper of my infirmity, to keep me in Your grace that I may never sin against You. Give me grace, O Holy Spirit, Spirit of the Father and the Son to say to You always and everywhere, "Speak Lord for Your servant heareth." Amen.

To be recited daily during the Novena: Prayer for the Seven Gifts of The Holy Spirit

O Lord Jesus Christ Who, before ascending into heaven did promise to send the Holy Spirit to finish Your work in the souls of Your Apostles and Disciples, deign to grant the same Holy Spirit to me that He may perfect in my soul, the work of Your grace and Your love. Grant me the Spirit of Wisdom that I may despise the perishable things of this world and aspire only after the things that are eternal, the Spirit of Understanding to enlighten my mind with the light of Your divine truth, the Spirit of Counsel that I may ever choose the surest way of pleasing God and gaining heaven, the Spirit of Fortitude that I may bear my cross with You and that I may overcome with courage all the obstacles that oppose my salvation, the Spirit of Knowledge that I may know God and know myself and grow perfect in the science of

the Saints, the Spirit of Piety that I may find the service
of God sweet and amiable, and the Spirit of Fear that I
may be filled with a loving reverence towards God and
may dread in any way to displease Him. Mark me, dear
Lord, with the sign of Your true disciples and animate
me in all things with Your Spirit. Amen.

(Holy Spirit Fathers, 1912)

Shorter Holy Spirit Novena

Dearest Holy Spirit, confiding in Your deep, personal
love for me, I am making this novena for the
following request, if it be Your Holy Will to grant it:
(*mention your request*).

Teach me, Divine Spirit, to know and seek my last end;
grant me the holy fear of God; grant me true contrition
and patience. Do not let me fall into sin. Give me an
increase of faith, hope and charity, and bring forth in my
soul all the virtues proper to my state in life.

Make me a faithful disciple of Jesus and an obedient
child of the Church. Give me efficacious grace
sufficient to keep the Commandments and to receive
the Sacraments worthily. Give me the four Cardinal
Virtues, Your Seven Gifts, Your Twelve Fruits. Raise me
to perfection in the state of life to which You have called
me and lead me through a happy death to everlasting
life. I ask this through Christ our Lord, Amen.

LITANIES FOR
~ CONSECRATED LIFE ~

Litanies are prayers of supplication consisting of a series of petitions addressed to a particular saint or to God. The following are litanies to St Benedict, St Francis of Assisi and St Ignatius of Loyola, three giant figures in the history of consecrated life.

Litany of St Benedict

Lord, have mercy on us. Christ, have mercy on us. Lord, have mercy on us; Christ, hear us. Christ, graciously hear us.

God the Father of Heaven, *have mercy on us.*
God the Son, Redeemer of the World, *have mercy on us.*
God the Holy Spirit, *have mercy on us.*
Holy Trinity, One God, *have mercy on us.*

Holy Mary, *pray for us.*
Holy Mother of God, *pray for us.*
Holy Virgin of Virgins, *pray for us.*

Holy Father St Benedict, *pray for us.*
Father most renowned, *pray for us.*

Father most affectionate, *pray for us.*
Father most patient, *pray for us.*
Father most merciful, *pray for us.*
Man of great fortitude, *pray for us.*
Man of venerable life, *pray for us.*
Disciplined man of prayer, *pray for us.*
Flower of piety, *pray for us.*
Flower of sanctity, *pray for us.*
Flower of chastity, *pray for us.*
Bright light of the world, *pray for us.*
Star of religion, *pray for us.*
Mirror of perfection, *pray for us.*
Teacher of silence, *pray for us.*
Example of poverty, *pray for us.*
Master of obedience, *pray for us.*
Paradigm of humility, *pray for us.*
Model of abstinence, *pray for us.*
Firm in faith, *pray for us.*
Strong in hope, *pray for us.*
Fervent in charity, *pray for us.*
Pure in mind, *pray for us.*
Chaste in body, *pray for us.*
Free from passions, *pray for us.*
Instrument of the miraculous, *pray for us.*
Revealer of the secrets of the heart, *pray for us.*
Foreknowing the future, *pray for us.*

Pattern of trust in the presence of evil, *pray for us.*
Confident in the Lord's providence, *pray for us.*
Adorned with the grace of God, *pray for us.*
Filled with the Holy Spirit, *pray for us.*
Raised to the height of angelic glory, *pray for us.*
Rapt in the ardour of contemplation, *pray for us.*
Joined to the choirs of angels, *pray for us.*
Exalted among the Patriarchs, *pray for us.*
Honoured among Abbots, *pray for us.*
Placed over the choir of Monks, *pray for us.*
Crowned with the lilies of Virgins, *pray for us.*
Patriarch of Western Monasticism, *pray for us.*
Patron of a happy death, *pray for us.*
Patron of many pontiffs, *pray for us.*
Patron of Europe, *pray for us.*
United to the company of all the Saints, *pray for us.*

Lamb of God, Who takes away the sins of the world, *spare us, O Lord.*
Lamb of God, Who takes away the sins of the world, *graciously hear us, O Lord.*
Lamb of God, Who takes away the sins of the world, *have mercy on us.*

V. Intercede for us, O holy Father, St Benedict
R. That we may be made worthy of the promises of Christ.

Let us pray:

O most holy Abbot Benedict, father and guide of monks, and intrepid warrior against evil, intercede for our salvation and the salvation of all mankind. Raise up, O Lord, in your Church the Spirit which animated St Benedict, and being filled with the same Spirit, may we seek to love what he loved and to practise what he taught. Grant us, we ask you O Lord, perseverance in doing your will, that in our days, the people serving you may increase both in dedication to prayer and in zeal for the Gospel. We ask this through Christ our Lord.

R. Amen.

Litany of St Francis of Assisi

Lord, have mercy on us.
Christ, have mercy on us.
Lord, have mercy on us.
Christ, hear us.
Christ, graciously hear us.

God the Father of Heaven, *have mercy on us.*
God the Son, Redeemer of the world, *have mercy on us.*
God the Holy Spirit, *have mercy on us.*
Holy Trinity, One God, *have mercy on us.*

Holy Mary, conceived without sin, *pray for us.*
Holy Mary, special patroness of the three Orders of
St Francis, *pray for us.*

St Francis, seraphic patriarch, *pray for us.*
St Francis, most prudent father, *pray for us.*
St Francis, despiser of the world, *pray for us.*
St Francis, model of penance, *pray for us.*
St Francis, conqueror of vices, *pray for us.*
St Francis, imitator of the Saviour, *pray for us.*
St Francis, bearer of the marks of Christ, *pray for us.*
St Francis, sealed with the character of Jesus, *pray for us.*
St Francis, example of purity, *pray for us.*
St Francis, image of humility, *pray for us.*
St Francis, abounding in grace, *pray for us.*
St Francis, reformer of the erring, *pray for us.*
St Francis, healer of the sick, *pray for us.*
St Francis, pillar of the Church, *pray for us.*
St Francis, defender of the Faith, *pray for us.*
St Francis, champion of Christ, *pray for us.*
St Francis, defender of thy children, *pray for us.*
St Francis, invulnerable shield, *pray for us.*
St Francis, confounder of the heretics, *pray for us.*
St Francis, converter of the pagans, *pray for us.*
St Francis, supporter of the lame, *pray for us.*
St Francis, raiser of the dead, *pray for us.*

St Francis, healer of the lepers, *pray for us.*
St Francis, our advocate, *pray for us.*

Lamb of God, Who takest away the sins of the world,
spare us, O Lord.
Lamb of God, Who takest away the sins of the world,
graciously hear us, O Lord.
Lamb of God, Who takest away the sins of the world,
have mercy on us.

Christ, hear us. Christ, graciously hear us.

V. Pray for us, O blessed St Francis
R. That we may be made worthy of the promises
    of Christ.

Let us pray:
O Lord Jesus Christ, Who, when the world was growing
cold, in order to renew in our hearts the flame of love,
imprinted the sacred marks of Thy Passion on the body
of St Francis, mercifully grant that by his merits and
prayers we may persevere in bearing the cross and may
bring forth fruits worthy of penance, Thou Who livest
and reignest, world without end.
R. Amen.

Litany of St Ignatius of Loyola

Lord, have mercy on us.
Christ, have mercy on us.
Lord, have mercy on us.
Christ, hear us.
Christ, graciously hear us.

God the Father of Heaven,
have mercy on us.
God the Son, Redeemer of the world,
have mercy on us.
God the Holy Ghost,
have mercy on us.

Queen of the Society of Jesus, *pray for us.*
St Joseph, Heavenly patron of the Society of Jesus,
pray for us.

St Ignatius, most devoted to the Blessed Trinity
pray for us.
St Ignatius, devoted son to our eternal Father,
pray for us.
St Ignatius, oracle of the Holy Spirit, *pray for us.*
St Ignatius, lover of Our Lord, *pray for us.*
St Ignatius, loyal knight of Our Lady, *pray for us.*
St Ignatius, founder of the Society of Jesus, *pray for us.*

St Ignatius, standard bearer of the King of kings,
pray for us.
St Ignatius, whose only ambition was to promote the
Kingdom of Christ and the greater glory of God,
pray for us.
St Ignatius, burning with zeal for the conversion
of unbelievers,
pray for us.
St Ignatius, intrepid foe of heresy and of the enemies
of Christ's Church,
pray for us.
St Ignatius, valiant and faithful champion of the Vicar
of Christ,
pray for us.
St Ignatius, like Our Lord in thy humility, *pray for us.*
St Ignatius, like Our Lord in thy modesty, *pray for us.*
St Ignatius, like Our Lord in thy obscurity, *pray for us.*
St Ignatius, like Our Lord in constant labours,
pray for us.
St Ignatius, like Our Lord in sympathy for the weak,
pray for us.
St Ignatius, like Our Lord in thy courage,
pray for us.
St Ignatius, consumed with a great desire for humiliation
with Our Lord,
pray for us.

St Ignatius, constant in the practise of corporal penance,
pray for us.
St Ignatius, staunch defender of poverty as the firm
wall of religion,
pray for us.
St Ignatius, lover of angelic purity and innocence,
pray for us.
St Ignatius, skilled master in the school
of holy obedience,
pray for us.
St Ignatius, living always in God's presence, *pray for us.*
St Ignatius, model of interior peace, *pray for us.*
St Ignatius, inspired writer of the Spiritual Exercises,
pray for us.
St Ignatius, patron of all retreats and retreat houses,
pray for us.
St Ignatius, victorious over the powers of darkness,
pray for us.
St Ignatius, holy father of many Saints and Martyrs,
pray for us.
St Ignatius, model of fervour to all priests, *pray for us.*
St Ignatius, burning with seraphic love at the Holy
Sacrifice of the Mass,
pray for us.

Lamb of God, Who takest away the sins of the world,
spare us, O Lord.
Lamb of God, Who takest away the sins of the world,
graciously hear us, O Lord.
Lamb of God, Who takest away the sins of the world,
have mercy on us, O Lord.

V. Pray for us, St Ignatius
R. That we may be made worthy of the promises of
Christ.

Let us pray:
O God, Who in Thy most merciful Providence didst call
Thy faithful servant, Ignatius of Loyola to a life of the
most exalted sanctity in the very close imitation of Thy
Divine Son, grant, we beseech Thee, that through his
powerful intercession, we may persevere in following in
the footsteps of this Thy servant until we breathe forth
our souls to Thee as faithful followers of Christ our King.
R. Amen.

REFLECTIONS FOR
~ CONSECRATED LIFE ~

The following reflections on the consecrated life come
from Pope St John Paul II and Pope Francis, and indicate
how highly they value the place of consecrated persons
in the life of the Church.

Edited from the Apostolic Exhortation
of Pope St John Paul II,
Redemptionis Donum, given on 25th March 1984

Religious profession creates a new bond between the
person and the One and Triune God, in Jesus Christ. It
is deeply rooted in baptismal consecration and is a fuller
expression of it. In this way religious profession, in its
constitutive content, becomes a new consecration: the
consecration and giving of the human person to God,
loved above all else.

The commitment undertaken by means of the vows
to practise the evangelical counsels of chastity, poverty
and obedience, is the expression of a total consecration
to God and, at the same time, the means that leads to
its achievement. This is also the source of the manner
proper to consecrated persons of bearing witness and of
exercising the apostolate.

It is not difficult to see the fundamental importance of the three evangelical counsels in the whole economy of Redemption. Evangelical chastity helps us to transform in our interior life everything that has its sources in the lust of the flesh; evangelical poverty, everything that finds its source in the lust of the eyes; and evangelical obedience enables us to transform in a radical way that which in the human heart arises from the pride of life. (cf. *1 Jn* 2:15-17)

Edited from the Message of Pope St John Paul II
for the First World Day for Consecrated Life,
given in March 1996

The mission of the consecrated life in the present and in the future of the Church, concerns not merely those who have received this special charism, but the entire Christian community.

The purpose of such a day is threefold: in the first place, it answers the intimate need to praise the Lord more solemnly and to thank him for the great gift of consecrated life, which enriches and gladdens the Christian community by the edifying fruits of so many lives totally given to the cause of the Kingdom.

In the second place, this day is intended to promote a knowledge of, and esteem for, the consecrated life by the entire People of God.

The third reason regards consecrated persons directly. They are invited to celebrate together solemnly the marvels which the Lord has accomplished in them.

Dear brothers and sisters, as I entrust to the maternal protection of Mary the institution of this World Day, I deeply hope that it bear abundant fruits for the holiness and the mission of the Church. May it help, in a special way, to heighten in the Christian community an esteem for vocations of special consecration, to stimulate ever more intense prayer for obtaining them from the Lord, in this way helping to mature in young people and families a generous willingness to receive them as gift. The life of the Church as a whole will draw benefit from this and so will the new evangelisation.

Edited version of the Address of Pope Francis to the participants in the Plenary Assembly of the International Union of Superiors General, given on Wednesday 8th May 2013

I would like to propose to you some simple thoughts: Jesus, at the Last Supper, turns to the Apostles with these words: "You did not choose me, but I chose you" (*Jn* 15:16). They remind us all that vocation is always an initiative of God. This means continuously making an "exodus" from ourselves in order to centre our life on Christ and on his Gospel, on the will of God, laying aside our own plans, in order to say with St Paul: "It is no longer I who live, but Christ who lives in me" (*Ga* 2:20).

If obedience is listening to the will of God, in the interior movement of the Holy Spirit authenticated by the Church - accepting that obedience also passes through human mediation - then poverty is overcoming every kind of selfishness, in the logic of the Gospel which teaches us to trust in God's Providence.

Poverty teaches solidarity, sharing and charity, and is also expressed in moderation and joy in the essential, to put us on guard against material idols that obscure the real meaning of life. A poverty learned with the humble, the poor, the sick and all those who are on the existential outskirts of life.

Then there is chastity, as a precious charism that broadens the freedom of our gift to God and to others, with tenderness, mercy, closeness to Christ.

It is impossible for a consecrated man or woman not to "think" with the Church. "Thinking" with the Church begot us at Baptism; "thinking" with the Church finds one of its filial expressions in faithfulness to the Magisterium, in communion with the Pastors and the Successor of Peter, the Bishop of Rome, a visible sign of unity.

No evangeliser acts, as Paul VI recalled very well, "in virtue of a…personal inspiration, but in union with the mission of the Church and in her name" (Apostolic Exhortation *Evangelii Nuntiandi*, n. 60).

From Pope Francis's *Regina Caeli* Address, 21st April 2013

Jesus wants to establish with his friends a relationship which mirrors his own relationship with the Father: a relationship of reciprocal belonging in full trust, in intimate communion. To express this profound understanding, this relationship of friendship, Jesus uses the image of the shepherd with his sheep: he calls them and they recognise his voice, they respond to his call and follow him.

The mystery of his voice is evocative: only think that from our mother's womb we learn to recognise her voice and that of our father; it is from the tone of a voice that we perceive love or contempt, affection or coldness. Jesus's voice is unique! If we learn to distinguish it, he guides us on the path of life, a path that goes beyond even the abyss of death.

However Jesus, at a certain point, said: "my Father, who has given them to me…" (*Jn* 10:29), referring to his sheep. If I feel drawn to Jesus, if his voice warms my heart, it is thanks to God the Father who has sown within me the desire for love, for truth, for life, for beauty… and Jesus is all this in fullness! This helps us understand the mystery of vocation and especially of the call to a special consecration.

Behind and before every vocation to the priesthood or to the consecrated life there is always the strong and intense prayer of someone: a grandmother, a grandfather, a mother, a father, a community… This is why Jesus said: "Pray therefore the Lord of the harvest," that is, God the Father, "to send out labourers into his harvest" (*Mt* 9:38).

Let us invoke the intercession of Mary who is the Woman of the "yes." Mary said "yes" throughout her life! She learned to recognise Jesus's voice from the time when she carried him in her womb. May Mary, our Mother, help us to know Jesus's voice better and better and to follow it, so as to walk on the path of life!

Scripture Related to
～ Consecrated Life ～

These readings from Scripture and from the Mass, as found in the New Testament, indicate just how important the themes associated with the evangelical counsels are for the life of the Church.

Scripture readings for Vocations to the Consecrated Life

Matthew 9:35-38 - on the need to pray for vocations

Jesus made a tour through all the villages and towns, teaching in their synagogues, proclaiming the Good News of the kingdom and curing all kinds of diseases and sickness. And when he saw the crowds he felt sorry for them because they were harassed and dejected, like sheep without a shepherd. Then he said to his disciples, "The harvest is rich but the labourers are few, so ask the Lord of the harvest to send labourers to his harvest."

Matthew 4:18-22 - on the need to respond to God's call

As Jesus was walking beside the Sea of Galilee, he saw two brothers, Simon called Peter and his brother Andrew. They were casting a net into the lake, for they were fishermen. "Come, follow me," Jesus said, "and I will send you out to fish for people." At once they left their nets and followed him. Going on from there, he saw two other brothers, James son of Zebedee and his brother John. They were in a boat with their father Zebedee, preparing their nets. Jesus called them, and immediately they left the boat and their father and followed him.

Mass readings related to the Consecrated Life

Matthew 13:44-46 - on the importance of sacrificing all for Christ

Jesus said to the crowds: "The kingdom of heaven is like treasure hidden in a field which someone has found; he hides it again, goes off happy, sells everything he owns and buys the field. Again, the kingdom of heaven is like a merchant looking for fine pearls; when he finds one of great value he goes and sells everything he owns and buys it."

Matthew 16:24-27 - on the importance of carrying our cross after Christ

Jesus said to his disciples, "If anyone wants to be a follower of mine, let him renounce himself and take up his cross and follow me. For anyone who wants to save his life will lose it; but anyone who loses his life for my sake will find it. What, then, will a man gain if he wins the whole world and ruins his soul? Or what has a man to offer in exchange for his soul? For the Son of Man is going to come in the glory of his Father with his angels, and, when he does, he will reward each one according to his behaviour."

Matthew 19:27-29 - on the importance of totally following Christ

Peter said to Jesus: "What about us? We have left everything and followed you. What are we to have, then?" Jesus said to him, "I tell you solemnly, when all is made new and the Son of Man sits on his throne of glory, you will yourselves sit on twelve thrones to judge the twelve tribes of Israel. And everyone who has left houses, brothers, sisters, father, mother, children or land for the sake of my name will be repaid a hundred times over, and also inherit eternal life."

Matthew 22:35-40 - on love of God and neighbour

To disconcert Jesus, one of the Pharisees, a lawyer, put a question, "Master, which is the greatest commandment of the Law?" Jesus said, "You must love the Lord your God with all your heart, with all your soul, and with all your mind. This is the greatest and the first commandment. The second resembles it:

you must love your neighbour as yourself. On these two commandments hang the whole Law, and the Prophets also."

*Luke 10:38-42 - on the superiority of
the contemplative life*

Jesus came to a village, and a woman named Martha welcomed him into her house. She had a sister called Mary, who sat down at the Lord's feet and listened to him speaking. Now Martha who was distracted with all the serving said, "Lord, do you not care that my sister is leaving me to do the serving all by myself? Please tell her to help me." But the Lord answered: "Martha, Martha," he said "you worry and fret about so many things, and yet few are needed, indeed only one. It is Mary who has chosen the better part; it is not to be taken from her."

*Luke 12:32-34 - on the importance of poverty
and almsgiving*

Jesus said to his disciples: "There is no need to be afraid, little flock, for it has pleased your Father to give you the kingdom. Sell your possessions and give alms. Get yourselves purses that do not wear out, treasure that will not fail you, in heaven where no thief can reach it and no moth destroy it. For where your treasure is, there will your heart be also."

*Acts of the Apostles 4:32-35 - on the importance
of communal life in the Church*

The whole group of believers was united, heart and soul; no one claimed for his own use anything that he had, as everything they owned was held in common. The apostles continued to testify to the resurrection of the Lord Jesus with great power, and they were all given great respect. None of their members was ever in want, as all those who owned land or houses would sell them, and bring the money from them, to present it to the apostles; it was then distributed to any members who might be in need.

*Ephesians 3:14-19 - on the primacy of love
in the spiritual life*

This is what I pray, kneeling before the Father, from whom every family, whether spiritual or natural, takes its name: Out of his infinite glory, may he give you the power through his Spirit for your hidden self to grow strong, so that Christ may live in your hearts through faith, and then, planted in love and built on love, you will with all the Saints have strength to grasp the breadth and the length, the height and the depth; until, knowing the love of Christ, which is beyond all knowledge, you are filled with the utter fullness of God.

*Philippians 4:4-9 - on the peace of mind that comes
from following Christ*

I want you to be happy, always happy in the Lord; I
repeat, what I want is your happiness. Let your
tolerance be evident to everyone: the Lord is very near.
There is no need to worry; but if there is anything you
need, pray for it, asking God for it with prayer and
thanksgiving, and that peace of God, which is so much
greater than we can understand, will guard your hearts
and your thoughts, in Christ Jesus. Finally, brothers, fill
your minds with everything that is true, everything that
is noble, everything that is good and pure, everything
that we love and honour, and everything that can be
thought virtuous or worthy of praise. Keep doing all the
things that you learnt from me and have been taught by
me and have heard or seen that I do. Then the God of
peace will be with you.

*Apocalypse 3:14, 20-22 - on the importance of
responding to God's call in our lives*

Here is the message of the Amen, the faithful, the
true witness, the ultimate source of God's creation:
"Look, I am standing at the door, knocking. If one of you
hears me calling and opens the door, I will come in to
share his meal, side by side with him. Those who prove
victorious I will allow to share my throne, just as I was

victorious myself and took my place with my Father on his throne. If anyone has ears to hear, let him listen to what the Spirit is saying to the churches."

Praying for
~ Consecrated Persons ~

Finally, these prayers should encourage us all to pray for vocations to the consecrated life, a life which is at the heart of the Church's mission to the world.

Hymn for Consecrated Life

My God, accept my heart this day

My God, accept my heart this day,
And make it always Thine,
That I from Thee no more may stray,
No more from Thee decline.

Before the cross of Him who died,
Behold, I prostrate fall;
Let every sin be crucified,
Let Christ be all in all.

Anoint me with Thy heavenly grace,
Adopt me for Thine own,
That I may see Thy glorious face,
And worship at Thy throne.

May the dear blood once shed for me
My blest atonement prove
That I from first to last may be
The purchase of Thy love!

Let every thought, and work, and word,
To Thee be ever given;
Then life shall be Thy service, Lord,
And death the gate of Heaven.

(Matthew Bridges, 1848)

Mass Prayers for Consecrated Life

Prayers of the Faithful

For those consecrated to God by the vows of chastity, poverty and obedience that they may seek to live their baptismal promises more intensely and have the grace to persevere in their commitment to the Lord and serve with open hearts and willing spirits.
We pray to the Lord…

For those who have responded to the prompting of the Holy Spirit to be a consecrated person that they may experience the support of the Church as they continue their growth in holiness.
We pray to the Lord…

We pray for those who are consecrated to God by the vows of chastity, poverty and obedience. May they always reveal the love of Christ to those they encounter and continue to enrich our world by their dedicated lives of prayer.
We pray to the Lord…

We pray for all those who are discerning their vocation in life, particularly those whom the Lord is calling to consecrated life. May they be given the wisdom to hear God's call and the courage to respond generously.
We pray to the Lord…

That God may give young men and women the gift of understanding to discern their service in the Church, the priesthood, diaconate, or consecrated life; and for the gift of courage to follow His call.
We pray to the Lord…

For young people; that they may know the personal love of the Lord for them, and respond with open and generous hearts.
We pray to the Lord…

Prayer for Consecrated Persons

God our Father, we thank you for calling men and women to serve in your Son's Kingdom as sisters, brothers, religious priests, consecrated virgins, and hermits, as well as members of Secular Institutes. Renew their knowledge and love of you, and send your Holy Spirit to help them respond generously and courageously to your will. We ask this through our Lord Jesus Christ, who lives and reigns with you and the Holy Spirit, one God, for ever and ever. Amen.